F-22 RAPTORS

BY DEREK ZOBEL

BELLWETHER MEDIA · MINNEAPOLIS, MN

Are you ready to take it to the extreme?
Torque books thrust you into the action-packed
world of sports, vehicles, and adventure. These books
may include dirt, smoke, fire, and dangerous stunts.
WARNING: read at your own risk.

Library of Congress Cataloging-in-Publication Data

Zobel, Derek, 1983-
 F-22 raptors / by Derek Zobel.
   p. cm. — (Torque: military machines)
 Includes bibliographical references and index.
 Summary: "Amazing photography and engaging information explain the technologies and
capabilities of the F-22 Raptors. Intended for students in grades 3 through 7"—Provided by
publisher.
 ISBN-13: 978-1-60014-204-8 (hardcover : alk. paper)
 ISBN-10: 1-60014-204-4 (hardcover : alk. paper)
 1. F/A-22 (Jet fighter plane)—Juvenile literature. I. Title.

 UG1242.F5Z62 2008
 623.74'64—dc22   2008019867

This edition first published in 2009 by Bellwether Media.

The photographs in this book are reproduced through the courtesy of the United States Department of
Defense.

Printed in the United States of America.

CONTENTS

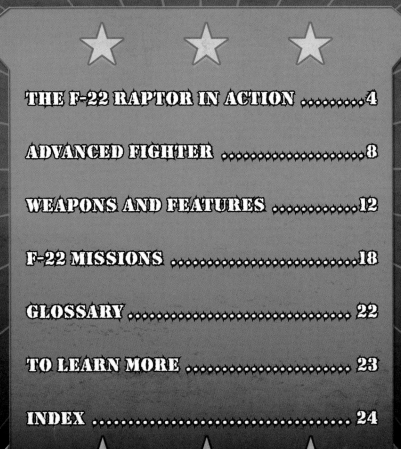

THE F-22 RAPTOR IN ACTION

Three F-22 Raptors streak through the sky. They're headed for a terrorist camp. The United States Air Force has learned that terrorists are about to launch an attack on the United States. The three F-22s fly in **formation** toward the enemy camp.

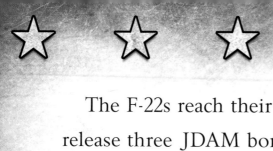

The F-22s reach their target. The pilots release three JDAM bombs. As the bombs strike, they light up the sky. The terrorist camp is destroyed. The F-22s have completed their **mission**.

The top speed of the F-22 is classified. Test pilots say it can go faster than 1,600 miles (2,575 kilometers) per hour.

ADVANCED FIGHTER

The F-22 Raptor is the U.S. Air Force's most advanced fighter. It entered U.S. Air Force service in December of 2005. It will be the standard fighter for the Air Force for years to come.

★ **FAST FACT** ★

The F-22 is replacing the F-117A Nighthawk.

The F-22's main role is **air superiority**. It is used to control the air in any battle with its great speed, handling, and advanced weaponry. The twin engines of the F-22 are the most powerful of any fighter in the world. They can push the F-22 to **supersonic** speeds. The F-22's great **maneuverability**, even at these speeds, makes it even more dominant in the air.

WEAPONS AND FEATURES

The **stealth** technology of the F-22 makes it invisible to enemy **radar**. Radar sends out radio waves to detect objects. The radio waves bounce off of objects and back to the sender. The F-22 deflects or absorbs these radio waves so they do not return to the sender.

weapons bays

All of the F-22's weapons are kept in internal weapons bays. If they were outside the plane, enemy radar would be able to detect them. The bays open when the F-22 is ready to fire.

F-22s can be armed for air-to-air missions and air-to-ground missions. In air-to-air missions, the F-22 carries six AIM-120 Advanced Medium Range Air-to-Air Missiles (AMRAAM) and two AIM-9 Sidewinder missiles. The F-22 carries two GBU-32 Joint Direct Attack Munitions (JDAM) in air-to-ground missions.

F-22 RAPTOR SPECIFICATIONS:

Primary Function: Air superiority

Length: 62 feet, 1 inch (18.9 meters)

Height: 16 feet, 8 inches (5.1 meters)

Wingspan: 44 feet, 6 inches (13.6 meters)

Speed: Classified

Range: 1,850 miles (2,977 kilometers)

Ceiling: Above 50,000 feet (15,240 meters)

Weight: 19,700 pounds (8,935 kilograms)

F-22 MISSIONS

The F-22 can perform a variety of missions. It can fight enemy planes, drop bombs on enemy targets, and **escort** other aircraft. Pilots plan their missions together and fly in formation to protect each other from threats.

★ FAST FACT ★

The F-22 has an M61A2 Vulcan cannon as a last-resort weapon. This gun has only 480 rounds, enough for five seconds of fire.

Radar, powerful jet engines, and stealth technology help the F-22 complete dangerous missions. The F-22 has powerful sensors and computer systems. It can track and shoot down enemy aircraft without being detected.

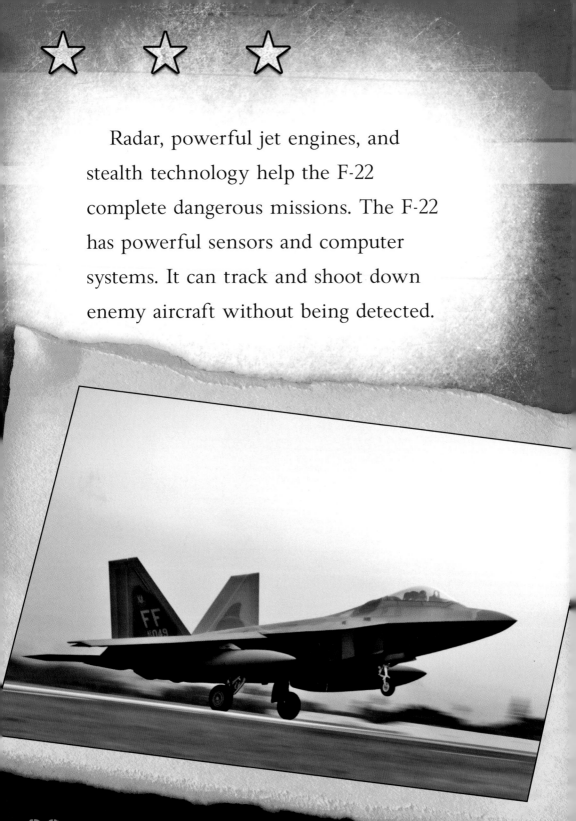

The air superiority of the F-22 has already been proven in several missions. Its advanced technology will help to protect the United States and its allies for years to come.

GLOSSARY

air superiority—the ability to counter any force in the air; the F-22's primary role is to control the air in any battle.

escort—to travel alongside and protect

formation—the pattern in which a group of planes fly

maneuverability—an aircraft's ability to change direction and speed

mission—a military task

radar—a sensor system that uses radio waves to locate objects

stealth—hidden

supersonic—able to move faster than the speed of sound

TO LEARN MORE

AT THE LIBRARY

Hansen, Ole Steen. *The F/A-22 Raptor*. Minneapolis, Minn.: Capstone, 2005.

White, Steve D. *Combat Fighter: F-22 Raptor*. New York: Children's Press, 2007.

Zobel, Derek. *United States Air Force*. Minneapolis, Minn.: Bellwether, 2008.

ON THE WEB

Learning more about military machines is as easy as 1, 2, 3.

1. Go to www.factsurfer.com

2. Enter "military machines" into search box.

3. Click the "Surf" button and you will see a list of related web sites.

With factsurfer.com, finding more information is just a click away.

INDEX